Bomb H

First published in Great Britain in paperback by Methuen 2019

1

Methuen & Co Ltd
Orchard House
Railway Street
Slingsby, York, YO62 4AN

www.methuen.co.uk

Methuen & Co Ltd Reg. No. 05278590

A CIP catalogue record for this title is available from the British Library

ISBN: 978 0 413 77822 2

Typeset by SX Composing DTP, Rayleigh, Essex

Printed and bound in Great Britain by Clays Ltd, Elcograf S.p.A.

Bomb Happy

A verbatim play

by
Helena Fox

in partnership with
York Normandy Veterans

Methuen

Acknowledgements

Grateful thanks to my son, Angus Fox, to Nick Beilby, Dorothy Bilton & Stephen Cooke, Mel Stansfield Glass, Sophie Buckley, Yvette Turnbull and to Laura Yeoman & Catriona Cannon at York Explore Library and Archive, where the York Normandy Veterans' Archive is held and, most importantly, the York Normandy Veterans, and wives & widows.

A word from the Veterans

Bomb Happy is a slang phrase we use for being under fire for many days at a time. It might sound a bit frivolous to use that term as the title for this play but it does describe the condition that you become.

We weren't really sure at the outset of the project back in 2016 how this play would work but it seemed a good idea to put our own words into a play in verbatim conversation, so that our experiences, and those of our comrades, could live on for future generations to read about, for young people to speak our words in performance, and through the performance to understand better the sacrifice so many made for our country's freedom, and the lifelong impact of conflict trauma.

By October 2017 we had sadly lost George Meredith and Dennis Haydock, but we three remaining veterans finally got to see it come to fruition on a sell-out tour in our home county, Yorkshire. And to have the play published to mark the 75th Anniversary of D-Day has been the icing on the cake.

These are our stories. Thank you for reading them.

Bert Barritt, Ken Smith, Ken Cooke
August 2018

Bomb Happy uses recorded interviews, written memoirs, official army and personal correspondence belonging to the five remaining York Normandy Veterans, along with testimonies by Veterans' wives and widows:

Mr Ken Smith	Private, 5th Battalion, Duke of Cornwall's Light Infantry
Mr Ken Cooke	Private, 7th Battalion, The Green Howards, and The Highland Light Infantry
Mr George Meredith	Private, Army Dispatch Rider with 11th Armoured Division
Mr Albert Barritt	Private, then Corporal, 2nd Battalion, East Yorkshire Regiment, 3 Yorkshire Division
Mr Dennis Haydock	Guardsman, Gunner in Sherman Tank, 2nd Battalion Coldstream Guards
Mrs Daphne Doran	York Normandy Veteran widow
Mrs Gloria Smith	Wife of Ken Smith

Author's note

It has been without doubt a most humbling experience to work with the last five remaining York Normandy Veterans and their families. The aim for us all at the outset of the project was to write a play that captured these soon to be lost first-hand accounts of D-Day & the Normandy Campaign, stories of five ordinary young men who found themselves part of one of the most important operations in military history. It became apparent during the interviews however that this wasn't just a play about those events as the veterans physically experienced them, but about the hidden world of long-term conflict trauma and survivor guilt – conditions that have affected the veterans ever since. Even now in their nineties, they are still haunted by memories of seeing their pals dying violent deaths on a near daily basis.

The memories contained in this play are a mere snapshot of just some of their wartime experiences – both amusing and traumatic. I hope this script will act as a lasting legacy not only to their memories, but to all those young men who lost their lives on the beaches of France and in liberating Europe. This play is for all of them, for we cannot know all their stories.

Creatives

Writer/Director	Helena Fox
Script dramaturgy	Alex Chisholm

Bomb Happy was first performed as three rehearsed readings in 2016 as part of North Yorkshire Moors' Railway in Wartime Festival, The Big City Read at York Explore Library and Archive and at The University of York with the following cast:

Smudger Smith	Angus Fox
Cookey	Sam McAvoy
Merry	Jack Fielding
Hank	Jack Chamberlain
Bert	Alfie Woodhead
Queenie	Beryl Nairn
Dramaturgy in rehearsal	Robbie Nestor

Bomb Happy was subsequently produced by Everwitch Theatre in partnership with Helmsley Arts Centre in 2017, touring to Helmsley Arts Centre, Georgian Theatre Royal Richmond, Square Chapel Halifax, Pocklington Arts Centre, Otley Courthouse & Junction, Goole. Cast:

Smudger Smith	Joe Sample
Cookey	George Stagnell
Merry	Carl Wiley
Hank	Adam Bruce
Bert	Thomas Lillywhite
Queenie	Beryl Nairn
Lighting Design	Steven Woolmer
Composer	Sam McAvoy
Set pieces	Gary Hancock

Bomb Happy was performed as part of the York Festival of Ideas 2019 at the York Army Museum from 14th June until 16th June with the following cast:

Smudger	Joe Sample
Cookey	Danny Mellor
Hank	Jack Chamberlain
Bert	William Darwin
Merry	Carl Wylie
Queenie	Beryl Nairn
Director	Helena Fox
Lighting Design	Steven Woolmar
Composer	Sam McAvoy
Set pieces	Gary Hancock

This production was commissioned by York Civic Trust to commemorate the 75th anniversary of the D-Day Landings.

Veterans Bert Barritt, Ken Smith and Ken Cooke, together with Gloria Smith, Daphne Doran, Elsie Johnson (George Meredith's partner) & Janet Barritt (Bert's wife), toured with the production meeting the audiences after the show. Sadly Dennis Haydock & George Meredith passed away before seeing the 2017 production realised.

A Note on the text

Bomb Happy is verbatim theatre. The words are taken from recorded interviews I made with the veterans, as well as from their previous recorded interviews, their personal & official correspondence, and the personal written memoirs of Dennis Haydock – all held in the York Normandy Veterans' Archive at York Explore Library and Archive.

The characters – Smudger, Cookey, Bert, Merry & Hank – are in real life Ken Smith, Ken Cooke, Albert Barritt, George Meredith and Dennis Haydock. The role of 'Queenie' is a fictional wife of a Normandy Veteran whom I have created from the interviews I undertook with the wives and widows of York Normandy Veterans.

I have transcribed the interviews word for word, trying to capture their individual accents, delivery, speech patterns and intonation. Any incorrect spellings, grammar or punctuation in the speeches are therefore deliberate.

At times during the interviews I noticed the veterans slipping from past to present tense when describing events, as if in that moment of recollection they were no longer safely in their living room at home, but back on the battlefield. It was in these moments that I saw the vulnerability of seventeen- and eighteen-year-old young men – as they were at the time – and, contrary to traditional verbatim theatre practice, this gave me the idea, when crafting the play, to present the characters at the age they were at conscription, not at the age of interview, and to therefore use the present tense throughout the script, heightening the immediacy of events being described.

Any staging should be as simple as possible to allow the focus to always be on the words as the actor delivers them. Verbatim words are precious.

Sometimes, in the text, when a speaker does not complete a sentence or changes direction of thought suddenly, I have written in brackets where I imagined the sentence was going. These are not intended to be spoken, merely to act as a guide to the actor in delivery. This proved helpful in rehearsal. Words shown in italic in square brackets are stage directions.

An oblique stroke [/] indicates that the next actor should begin performing his line, thus overlapping the original speaker.

In performance the scenes should flow in and out of each other, continuously building momentum, driving the story forward, echoing the relentless nature of war.

Once the five soldiers enter they should remain on stage at all times. Actors should be cast age appropriately.

Characters

Smudger Smith	an eighteen-year-old, Ken Smith, from Armley in Leeds
Cookey	eighteen-year-old Ken Cooke, born Nottinghamshire, growing up in York
Merry	sixteen-year-old George Meredith, an East End lad from Stratford, London
Hank	eighteen-year-old Dennis Haydock, from Sheffield
Bert	eighteen-year-old Albert Barritt, a 'Bermondsey Boy' from London
Queenie	late eighties, a Veteran's wife or widow from Yorkshire

One
Home, England

Darkness. Haze gently covers the floor – the mist of time mixed with the smoke of battlefield.

The stage is bare except for a large army crate situated upstage. Inside this crate will be stored various smaller ration crates and ammo crates. Throughout the play the conscripts will use the different sized crates much as children would use blocks when playing – to build objects – the driving seat of a lorry, the inside of a tank or to mark out a two-man trench. They will do this with speed and military precision to allow smooth transitions and to not interrupt the flow of the piece.

The sound of a young child's voice/children's voices can be heard, as if carried in on the breeze, singing the old nursery rhyme The Grand Old Duke of York. *As the song fades away the sound of children laughing can just be heard as if playing a game, full of fun.*

At the same time lighting reveals **Queenie** *in spotlight, lost in thought, remembering*

Queenie   Me and me husband we was at Arramanche – I remember it very well, all the York Normandy Vets all went over to France, for the Fiftieth Anniversary, D-Day you know, there were a lot more of them still alive then – and me & me husband we was at Arramanche and there was two parties of school children there, having their lunch, and me 'usband was . . . he was very quiet . . . he was stood up looking out to sea, and the teacher came over to me and said "Can we ask, was your husband here during war?" So I said, "Oh yes, on this beach!" So this teacher went back, told the other teacher, got

Queenie (*cont.*) all the children together and said about
this gentleman that had come back. And they surrounded
him, these children. Thanking him. Thanked him they
did, "Merci Monsieur" you know? – because of him they
were . . . having this lovely life, sort of thing. And he
broke down completely, and I got down on my knees
down side of 'im to say (it's ok) – and 'e said "Nobody
'as any idea at all, nobody, the horrors that I've seen. I
want to go home. I don't want to ever come 'ere again,
or even talk about it again!" and 'e just clammed up.
Kept it to 'isself.

I can't even begin to imagine what 'e saw. I don't think
anybody can ever explain – no matter how old these
Veterans get each year, and what they tell you – I don't
know how anyone of us can actually experience what,
what they went through. The things they saw. The things
they had to. Things they were made to do. No choice.
Every single one of 'em says that.

Conscription.

No choice.

And they were just bairns really . . . not much more than
children themselves. Just ordinary kids...

[*Light fades on* **Queenie** *as the sound of marching footsteps
approach*]

[*Exit* **Queenie**

Enter **Bert**, **Cookey**, **Hank**, **Merry** *and* **Smudger**

[*Lights reveal the five young conscripts marching, whistling* The
Grand Old Duke of York. **Bert**, **Cookey**, **Hank**, **Merry** *and*
Smudger *may march through the auditorium or enter from the
opposite wings to where* **Queenie** *has left the stage. They should
march with energy, vitality. The soldiers are fresh-faced, full of
youthful energy and excitement*]

[**Bert, Cookey, Hank, Merry** *and* **Smudger** *unpack the large army crate as they whistle. They do this with military precision, working as a team to open and retrieve and pass the smaller crates inside to each other. They stack the crates centre stage creating a low stand, using some of the crates to build a step or staircase up to it.* **Merry,** *the youngest conscript, a lad of sixteen, will step up onto the stand once the crates are in place*]

[**Merry,** *the youngest conscript – a lad of sixteen – climbs onto the 'stand.'* **Bert, Cookey, Hank** *and* **Smudger** *stand to attention around him*]

[*Soundtrack underscores* **Merry**'s *attestation.*[1]]

Merry I, George Edward Meredith, swear by Almigh'y God that I will be faithful and bear true allegiance to His Majesty King George the Sixth, 'is 'eirs, and Successors, and that I will, as in duty bound, 'onestly and faithfully defend 'is Majesty, 'is 'eirs, and Successors, in Person, Crown and Dignit-y against all enemies, and will observe and obey all orders of 'is Majesty, 'is 'eirs and Successors, and of the Generals and Officers set over me, this the Seventh day of May 1941. [*Salutes*]

[*Soundtrack fades out as* **Merry** *jumps down from the crates and addresses the audience.* **Bert, Cookey, Hank** *and* **Smudger** *no longer stand to attention and join him. They are excited and this excitement and energy increases throughout their dialogue, each speech building on the last. The five soldiers may find moments within the dialogue to use the assembled crates almost like a playground, to express their youthful exuberance and excitement, to demonstrate, to climb up on, jump from etc*]

Merry [*addressing the audience directly, excitedly*] Me name's Merry – they can't pronounce me name in my battalion – Meredith [*laughs*] – so they all call me Merry! And this 'ere is Smudger.

---

1 Merry's Attestation can be found in the York Normandy Veterans' Archive

Smudger Everyone has a nickname in the army, you know? And being Smith I'm called Smudger – Smudger Smith, Chalky White, you know that sort of thing! A Yorkshire lad. But they put me in the Duke of *Cornwall's* Light Infantry – they couldn't get any further away than that could they?

Bert [*laughing*] And I'm a Londoner, and put in the *Yorkshires*! A Bermondsey boy! As a child I see Tower Bridge every day. I'm Bert, by the way, and this /is . . .

Cookey /Cookey's the name! I'm in the Green (H)oward's! I'm an Infantryman like Smudger and Bert 'ere, you know, what they call the P.B.I . . .

Smudger / Bert / Cookey The Poor Bloody Infantry!

Cookey I grow up in East Kirby, Nottingham, before we come'a York – so a small mining village. Me father's a miner.

Bert Father works on the docks. Mother's scrapes a living from her dressmaking.

Hank My father's a grinder – in the steelworks. [*Salutes*] Hank the Tank Haydock that's me! They used to call me 'H-addock.' Now you'd think being a H-addock I'd be able to swim wouldn't you, but I can't. [*Laughs*] So now it's 'Hank'. I don't really know why. Rhymes with tank I suppose.

I live in Sheffield, in a back to back house in what they called Addis Street. And it's a very poor . . . me mother and father are poor. And they can't speak properly, they're deaf *and* dumb – but I manage to communicate with them on my fingers.

Bert: *My* mother's deaf actually – and so's father. Met at deaf school.

Merry [*climbing up the steps/crates to demonstrate the height of the building*] The 'ouse we live in is three, four stories high, but we're down in the basement – just off the Stratford High Road. Me and me brother – and me Uncle Tom now lives with us, and e', e's a boxer! Oh yeah! Many a time mother come 'ome and 'e 'as me 'angin' out the window by me . . . [*laughs*] feet!

Cookey [*pushing* **Merry** *off the crates as he climbs up himself*] We kids go to the local, we have like a . . . a recreation ground with all the swings and er seesaws and all that there. We play football and cowboys and Indians and we really enjoy that you know? One day you're a cowboy, next day you're an Indian. We get all the bumps and scrapes and everything and what the grown-ups say is, "Ah, that's nothing, go and play again!" . . . and off we go!

[**Cookey** *emits a 'cowboy and Indians' style war cry. He jumps off the crates as he does so and chases* **Bert** *who takes refuge behind the crates*]

Smudger Move about a bit, 'cos my father likes the south – leave Leeds and live in Bournemouth, live in Brighton, live in Ashford in Kent – we're on the flightpath for the German planes heading for London and so we watch the Battle of Britain from our back garden!

Bert [*popping up from behind the crates and scrambling on top of them*] I'm in the Boys' Brigade – I play the drum – play in the Albert Hall one day. [*Marching down the crates as he speaks, and miming bashing a drum*] Our grand bandmaster marches us down the steps and the bugles play and I play the drums. I can't remember the tune we play. Well, with drumming sometimes you make your own! [*Laughs*]

Smudger Me and my pal Derek go on our bicycles down to Dover and stand on the cliffs and watch the German Stuka dive bombers bombing the shipping going through the channel there. And if an aircraft's shot down – a German plane – we get on our cycles and we try to beat the police – and the military – to the crash site. And if we get there before them, we take souvenirs – bits and pieces of aircraft!

[*A whistle is blown.* **Bert**, **Cookey**, **Hank**, **Merry** *and*
Smudger *quickly 'fall in']*

Merry Never think about what I want to do with me life
when I'm growing up. Nothin', never think about that.
You don't look ahead, you only look what the day is. Live
each day as it come and –

[*Whistle blows again.* **Bert**, **Cookey**, **Hank**, **Merry** *and*
Smudger *stand to attention]*

Merry I'm sixteen when I sign up. I want to sign up!
Yeah! I volunteer. I mean me two mates want to go as
well, and Bill says "I'm going!" – so we says "If you're
going, we're going!" I mean the only en(t)ertainment
we got 'ere in Stratford is goin' down the rec, so we think
it's an adventure. And we goes to Wicks Cross, the other
side of Wanstead Flats, and Bill signs up first, and I goes
second and mate Stooart come third. They don't do no
checks or nothing, if you're willing to go you're willing
to go, they just take me word for it that I'm eighteen.
[*Pulls himself up tall*] I'm as big as Bill is so they just look
us and say "Sign here!" So I sign here and "There's
your shilling," and then they say "You're a soldier in the
army!" [**Merry** *puffs up, proudly*] They kit us all out and
that, me and Bill and Stooart. In our uniforms and all
that! And we march through town! And where do we go
to start our soldier training? To West Cliff High School
for *Girls!* [*Bursts out laughing*] We end up in a bloody
girls' school! [*Laughs*]

Cookey 1943, December, just before Christmas when
they send me the letter saying "Come 'ere, we want ya!"
Eighteen yeah. Go up to Richmond, me mum and dad
come down to the station, see me off. Have a little attaché
case, battered it is, it's been in the family years sort of
thing, you know, sort of thing I can carry me gear in and
go up to Richmond. We start our six-week training then.

Hank I'm not worried about being called up or going to
fight.

Bert I think most of us are looking forward to the excitement!

Hank Being called up for the army – being in the army is a relief . . . in some respects . . . 'cos I leave me mother and father behind. And of course I don't like doing that – I'm sad to leave me mother because me mother being deaf has to rely on me quite a lot – but in some ways it's a *relief* . . . it don't stop me from going.

Bert I take the line it's an order from the Government so I'm happy to do it – in spite of my faith.

[*During the next speech* **Smudger**'s *excitement recedes as the reality of conscription in practice and what it will entail hits him*]

Smudger I know nothing, very little about the political situation – I know there's a chap called Hitler who isn't a very nice gentleman, but we don't know, we don't know much about what's going on and the second I enter the barrack – I come from a good Christian family, I don't mean a religious family like Bert, but I'm not . . . streetwise, I don't run the streets, and the *second* I'm in the army I'm taught to kill – kill with weapons, without weapons – it's surprising – you don't know how easy it is to kill a person without a weapon. It's frightening to think how easy it is to, to kill a person, or with a knife if you wanted – and I hope I never, I hope *I* never have to.

[*The soundtrack kicks in again, ominously driving forward as:*

Two
D-Day Approaches

June 1944

[*Lighting crossfades slowly to reveal an early summer's evening*]

Bert, **Cookey**, **Hank**, **Merry** *and* **Smudger** *each take a crate or box (making up the 'stand') and find their own space in which to sit*

[**Bert**, **Cookey**, **Hank**, **Merry** *and* **Smudger** *are oblivious to each other now, each sitting in different army camps across the country waiting to be sent to France*]

[**Merry** *and* **Hank** *may sit in shadow, but the audience is aware of them*

Bert After six weeks' training in the Fusiliers I'm posted to Richmond and I'm rubbing my 'ands thinking Richmond, Surrey! That's good! That's near 'ome. Might get a chance of nipping 'ome at the weekends! . . . Turns out it's only Richmond, *Yorkshire* – I've been posted to the East Yorks Regiment! . . . Have to learn a whole new language! [*Secretively*] Then, three weeks, three weeks before Normandy start, they lock us in the camps, and we can't get out. I'm transferred to a camp outside, outside Portsmouth – [*remembers*] – Waterlooville. There's no leave, no passes. And every letter is censored. [*Beat*] But then, suddenly, they begin to tell you what's happening. They begin to give you information.

Cookey [*jumping up to demonstrate*] Sergeant says "Right lads, there's an officer further down and he'll show you what you're gonna do." And there's uh three or four trestle tables laid out with all photographs of French coast, Normandy coast. Two hundred of us all trying to jump up and get a look at these photographs, you can imagine we we're sort of, "Shift out, let's have a look!" sort of thing. That's when we know . . . we're told we're gonna land in France.

Smudger Oh yes, last minute. We know it's Normandy – but where Normandy is I've no idea! I'm reasonably – although I left school at fourteen and a half, I've a reasonable education but um – I don't realise, I don't tie it up with 1066, I've no idea where Normandy is.

Cookey People have asked me about this and I'm not frightened, I'm not, er, scared or anything like that it's just the adventure to me – we never been on a ship before, but we're 'ere in Southampton, we see all these ships, think you know, "Oh lovely, all these big ships, ooh look-a it!"

Bert My watch word is 'I'm in God's hands.' I'm not expecting him to save my life but I'm in his hands for whatever it is he wants.

Smudger [*stands, preparing himself*] 5th June – we're boarding this ship in Newhaven – an old coastal steamer – and this is it. We're under no illusion. If this invasion fails, there'll be no second chance – we'll be under Nazi rule.

[*Beat*] [*A distorted, grinding sound permeates briefly*]

[*Lights cross fade to show early morning, the dawn. The lighting effect may create the image of water surrounding* **Cookey** *and* **Smudger**]

[**Bert** *is now in shadow, along with* **Hank** *and* **Merry**

[*A whistle blows*]

[*The following speeches by* **Cookey** *and* **Smudger** *build in urgency, as if the two actors are relay racers continually passing a baton between each other, building and keeping the momentum going, the flow and nervous energy of delivery never dipping as the beach landings progress, until finally they get off the beach / stop for the night. The pull of traumatic memory drags the two soldiers from the 'here and now' – at times they are no longer 'remembering' but back there unable to take their eyes off events unfolding around them, reliving the experience as if it is happening right now. They should 'see' the beach ahead of them, pinpointing its location. This focus should drive the speeches forward throughout. When one soldier is speaking, the other soldier will remain still – his energy maintained, and his focus on the beach ahead/ the top of the beach and safety*]

Cookey [*instantly responding to whistle*] "Everybody up!" Half past four in morning – D-Day – fast asleep in our bunks and the announcement's coming out the loudspeakers! Go into the mess, scotch porridge with salt, not sugar, salt, horrible stuff it is, corned beef sandwich and a tot of rum. Get all your weapons together and your pack and everything, get ready and we're all up on the deck, and there's a certain time six or seven miles from the coast we have to scramble down the nets into the landing craft . . . we're all a bit scared 'cause the landing craft are up and down like that, and we're having to time it where you drop off the landing net into the landing craft. [*Beat*] And now we're all in like, all ready, and we're setting off towards the beach.

Smudger There's nearly seven thousand vessels in the channel – there's four and a half thousand landing craft, a thousand odd naval vessels, uh, um, submarines, there's thousands of aircraft flights . . . I mean the noise is uh, the noise is um well horrific, and yet onboard the landing craft it's silent. People are even whispering. It's funny is this – there's all that noise going on and yet you're whispering on board. It's almost complete silence – um because although we're maybe rough and ready and irreligious, we're all praying to the Almighty for deliverance, on this day, on the British boats. I mean we have a padre on our boat, and they're quite literally queuing up to be blessed by him – people who would never probably go to church. Normally.

Cookey The battleships and all the, er, explosions start you know – they're firing at the beaches, rockets, smoke, noise, you've never heard anything like it you know? As we're approaching the beaches quite a few of us are being sea sick because up and down like this you know, but I'm not, I'm that excited that I'm leaning on the side of the ship watching all the fireworks going off you know? thinking "This is interesting . . ."

Smudger We're all terrified, yes. But, we want to get ashore because if we're only slightly wounded getting off the boats, we sink. The weight of the equipment – we've got on about sixty pounds worth of equipment – it'll just take us to the bottom – I'll just drown.

[*The watery effect will slowly fade as* **Cookey** *speaks. Haze representing the smoke of battlefield may begin to filter across the stage*]

Cookey As we're getting, er, near to the er, beach we see the cross pieces – mines – quite a few explode and destroy the other landing craft . . . [*stops*] and suddenly we're bumping into one of these – [*relieved*] but for some reason it doesn't go off. [*Beat*] Ours doesn't go off. [*Building*] We're carrying on onto the beach, and some of the other landing crafts don't get in as far as we do, there's a strong current, there's a strong current this side of the channel and it builds the sand up underneath, builds a sandbank like this under the water. Now the landing craft is hitting that bank and is thinking "Oh we're at the beach. Drop the ramps!" The chaps are jumping off and straight down into about twenty foot of water, ten foot, twenty foot of water, with all their gear . . . (they) don't stand a chance. But we're very lucky. I'm very lucky because I land in about six inches of water – we're right up on the beach, and there's some people, even the tank

Cookey (*cont.*) landing craft, they think they've landed – but no, the tanks are rolling off and they're going straight down. No chance for people inside the tanks whatever. People inside don't stand a chance. We get right up onto the beach, drop the landing ramp, step off and I'm stepping off into about this much water – just getting me socks wet, you know? "Ugh! Look at that! I've wet all me sock." That's just how I feel. I ain't bothered about explosions – wet socks, that's all I'm bothered about, you know?

Smudger The ramp goes down and we're getting machine guns – I mean the German machine guns are firing twice the rate of ours, about fourteen hundred rounds a minute compared with our seven hundred, and getting – the thing is, to get ashore quick as possible and get off the beach because it's just full of shells, mortar bombs & rockets – all I can see is the sand spurting up and I know that there's mines all the way up on the beach. So even though the Royal Engineers as they've come ashore have put some tapes down where they're clearing mines, they can't clear everything – there's so many and the next thing I see is body parts flying in the air, and I know . . . I'm in the minefield.

Cookey We have to get off the (beach), people are falling and they aren't getting up again, you know? It's just, as kiddies we were used to playing Indians and cowboys, you fall down then get up and you changes sides, you be an Indian one day and a cowboy another day, that sort of thing, you know, but these chaps are falling and they aren't getting up again, it's the real thing, these bullets are real.

Smudger I mean I haven't seen anybody dead before, and we're in the water wading to the shore, and we're literally brushing against what looks like logs and they're just bodies rolling in the surf – people that we know! Eighteen, nineteen, twenty-year olds! They're people that we know.

Cookey But you aren't allowed to stop once you get on the beach you aren't allowed to stop on the beach, you have to keep going – if anybody falls, you don't, whether it's your pal or anything, you leave them to the medics.

Smudger There's one of our chaps, there's a nineteen year old lad, a Cockney lad, in our company, he's a stockily built little Cockney, bombastic, bragging, um, he's afraid of nobody and nothing, and he struts about, he doesn't walk, he swaggers, telling anybody who will listen to 'im he's frightened of nothing and nobody and how he runs rings round the police when he runs with this gang in London. I'm literally shaking – with fear, not shivering, shaking on the assault boats, and all of a sudden I feel a hand on my shoulder, and I think it must be an officer or a senior NCO coming to tell me to pull myself together, and when I look round it's this little cockney lad. And he says in a shaky voice, he says "I'm scared mate" – after all this! So I just says to him "We'll stick together, look after each other." And I stop shaking. I mean I feel I have to set an example. And immediately the ramp goes down, bop down into the water met with (heavy machine gunning) – we're getting it from the left flank . . . And we're zigzagging up the – where the tapes have been put down by the Royal Engineers – supposedly safe ground, and out of the corner of my eye, the little cockney lad goes down – he's down – and you're not allowed to stop. You do automatically – reflex – just hesitate and this voice from behind is shouting "Keep going, lad!" And I have no choice. I have to keep going. You get to the top of the beach, there's a drainage ditch that runs down and that's where we re-group, at the, on the drainage ditch. And um, we get to this um, like a drainage ditch, an officer, our officer is there waiting for me. I'm carrying the wireless set, and the officer's shouting "Signaller!" and I hand him the microphone. Next thing I hear words I've never heard before, I learn some choice words as the air turns blue because it doesn't work! The radio isn't working. And now he has me stripping the set down in the midst of the landing battle, in the middle of the beach I'm having to find myself a little scrape in the

Smudger (*cont.*) sand and take, start taking the receiver and transmitter to pieces, and I'm taking the receiver out, and there's a machine gun bullet lodged in the receiver and one in the battery! [*Half laugh*] The radio has saved my life! [*Builds urgently*] But he's sending me *back!* I'm to go back and find a *dead* signaller. All the traffic, all the vehicles, all the people coming up the beach and me trying to go – they're thinking I'm trying to run away! Because we passed one of our signallers that I knew on the way up, that was laid, um that had been killed – and I'm having to roll him over and take the receiver out the back of his set, his wireless and his sound valves off him. And I've never handled or seen anything that has – this is the first time I've seen anybody . . . violent death, you know?

Cookey We carry on, we have to get off the beaches as quickly as possible. We follow up through our 6th Battalion. They land Thursday at half past seven, we land at quarter to eight and they carry on first do the 6th, and get in their positions. And when we land we carry on, we go through their positions, clear a village, and then they came through us, we clear a village, they clear a village, we carry on – any mopping up to do we do after the 6th have gone, any mopping up to do they clear up after *we've* gone. [*Beat/relief*] Our regiment we get the furthest on D-Day, I think we cross the railway line that goes to Cannes and we're having to pull back because we've gone too far . . . we're scared of being cut off so we have to pull back. And this is the first (day) and this the furthest point of this day we reach and we've gone too far, we're having to pull back.

Smudger They get as far as Bayeux the first day – that's the first town to be liberated in France, but all we're having to do is re-group and try and find the rest of our unit. So we're just making our way cautiously about half a mile and uh, then we dig in.

[*Light crossfades to night time*]

[*A distorted sound peppers* **Cookey***'s speech, underscoring from time to time*]

Cookey We settle in for the night. And we're watching the German planes coming over to see if they can bomb the harbour where we've landed you know? But there's only one or two. And we can see 'em up there, we can see the searchlights going on with the anti-aircraft and there's this thing they call Monty's Moonlight – Montgomery – they call it his moonlight – it's like daylight, all the searchlights on the horizon hundreds of searchlights. And, er, we're asking, er, where's Jim? where's Harry? Oh, he got killed. You're lookin' for your mates sort of thing and they aren't there, you say what happened to...? Have you seen him? Oh, he got killed – that's the conversation that's going on and, er, it's a bit, er, when the following day you realise what's happening, you don't realise what's happening on D-Day, everything's exciting you know, never been anything like it before, it's just a big adventure to us young . . . young lads and suddenly it's getting serious for us you know, we've seen things that we shouldn't have done sort of thing you know. You join up with the fellas and you go for a drink while you was over there in England and all play football and all the rest of it with the regiment and get to know them and everything and when somebody says So and So's been killed – Oh, I used to play football with him.

Smudger I never found out if the Cockney lad was just wounded or killed or anything. I mean there's been what, twelve and a half thousand casualties on D-Day? Four and a half thousand British killed on this one day.

Cookey You know after all this happens you realise what you've seen and what you've been through sort of thing, you know? And it really upsets you. You then, you feel a bit scared because the adrenaline isn't there then, it's got serious . . . you've seen your friends killed.

> [*Lights crossfade to reveal a new dawn as the*
> *soundtrack drives forward into darker*
> *dangerous waters, until it hits safer stream and . . .*

Three
Heading Inland

[*We see and hear* **Merry** *whistling the song* Wish me luck as you wave me goodbye! *as he goes about his job delivering supplies or ammo to the troops. Whilst he speaks he picks up some heavy ration boxes from around the stage and carries them on his shoulder to another area where he will stack them regimentally.*

[**Bert, Cookey, Hank** *and* **Smudger** *are in shadow*

Merry When they transferred me to the Royal Army Service Corps I hadn't droven before but I passed first time! Corporal has a go at me he does, 'cos I says I've never droven before. "You're a liar!" he says, "you've drove before!" I says "I 'avent!" and I 'adnt! I hadn't drove nothing before, but it just seemed to come natural. You see I'm a driver now. [*Breaking off from his work to explain*] We *was* all in the rifle brigade, all together, me, Bill & Stooart, doing our six-week training, and then Monty's taken over the training and he wants it more mobile, so 'e breaks the Battalion up, breaks the Battalion up, and Bill goes, 'e goes in the Tank Corps. But uh, Stooart stops in the rifle brigade. 'e manages to stop in there, I dunno why or 'ow 'e gets stopped in there, and they shove *me* into uh Royal Army Service Corps where, like I say, I become a driver. [*Pause*] We didn't like it much, being broken up, me and Bill and Stooart, you know? but wasn't much we could do about it. [*Laughs softly*] Can't fight all the army! [*Wheezy laugh*] So we just get out – and then I never see 'em no more, after that. [*Wistfully*] Never see 'em again. [*Pause*] Over 'ere I just do what the sergeant tell me. I take the supplies to a destination, what they do with it, I don't bother about. I don't transport petrol no more – now they've set a pipe up under the channel.

[**Merry** *stands up and goes to collect another ration box to add to the new stack*]

Merry There was three of us come over with petrol – on D-Day Plus One, yeah? [*Starts laughing*] We's loading, we's loading the trucks – on D-Day this is – and puttin' 'em in the hold down in King Edward Docks, King Edward Docks in London, ready to go to France. And we don't know – we're doing exercises and training and that, but now we don't know whether we's still doing exercises or whether we're in the war like, you know, 'til they put us on this boat! They put me on this boat and it's now I realise something's happening! [*Beat*] First time ever I've been outta this country, D-Day! Only ferry I ever been on is on the Thames – a penny bus ride from where we live! But if the old sergeant says "You do that, you cross the Channel!" whether you want to or not, like, you do it, no arguments . . . and when they lift me (truck) up – I'm not in it [*laughs*] – they lift it up to lower it into the hold and the Captain of the boat comes out and 'e says "I don't want that on 'ere!" 'e says, "that's got a petrol leak – I can smell it!" So off! 'e won't put us on! Well, I've got over a thousand gallon o' petrol on the back in jerry cans! That's why 'e can smell it! [*Wheezy laughter*] I'm thinking now what am I gonna do, I gotta get over to France! – and fortunately the Canadians are there, and they have an odd boat that isn't full up, so they take me. And so we go on the landing crafts 'cos nobody else will 'ave us! [*Beat*] We catch the tide right, cause we's well up. [*A distorted grinding sound permeates momentarily*] And they drop you, drop the front and off we go. And I'm driving onto Juno Beach. It's still a dangerous situation even on Day Two – there's still some mines on the beach – and I'll go with a bang if I go up – with a thousand gallon o' petrol on the back! The Red Caps are there and they're directing. You just keep your foot down and get out the bloody way . . . [*loudly/laughing*] get off the bloody beach!

Merry *freezes in action at the end of his speech*

Bert *steps out of shadow*

[*For* **Bert** *it is still the early hours of D-Day. In a separate area to* **Merry**, **Bert** *uses a couple of ammo crates to create the side of a ship, which he then stands on, precariously. He is now on board a ship approaching Sword Beach, waiting to jump. Sporadic sounds of mines exploding or distorted sounds underscore his speech*]

[**Cookey, Hank, Merry** *&* **Smudger** *are in shadow*

Bert D-Day, approaching Sword Beach. This is it, this is what we've trained for – back home – along the Moray Firth, landing a number of times, the ramp coming down, you jump in the water and [*mimes holding his rifle up*] – in the camp we've even taken quite a space to mark out the beach and the roads up from the beach so we'll know where we're going – and now, this is it . . . D-Day – when suddenly they're keeping a number of us back – keeping us back as 'immediate reinforcements.' [*Looks shocked*] L.O.B! Left out of battle! I'm thinking "We trained for this and now it's not gonna happen!" But I'm in God's hands. It may be a disappointment to me, but it's not my will, it's God's will. So, that's how it is. That's helped me in a lot of situations. Yes. So that's how it is.

[*Beat*]

Bert The Battalion land at H-hour, 7.30 am, in the First Wave and should have fought their way forward, clearing the beach of enemy. And now 10.30 am we're approaching Sword Beach – as immediate reinforcements. There's noise everywhere, all around us, noise coming from our boats, noise from above – because the Navy are out here firing guns over us. Noise. The noise! And we're landing in the same place on the right-hand side but not in the same way as the others, 'cos, as 'immediate reinforcements' we're on a big ship and we can walk down the side and jump into the water holding up our rifles and wade to shore . . . [*remembering, finding comfort in the memory*] wading to shore – just like on the Thames, in Bermondsey, where we played as children. You don't call it a beach! On a river – it's a *shore*. [*Laughs*] As kids we used to play along the shore and get our boots muddy, [*laughing*] and then go home to face Mother – oh dear! [*Shakes himself out of reminiscence with what he sees around him*] And now we're wading ashore – and in one way I'm pleased I'm not in the First Wave. We're seeing some of the wounded, some of the people we know wounded. Um our padre has been wounded, he's sitting on the, he's sitting up against the wall, on the floor with a damaged arm. We want to get off quick, er you know? So we're walking off the beach, but the trouble is, we're walking all day because we don't meet up with the First Wave. It was a very noisy day. And we're seeing, I mean, people, bodies and of course animals on farms – dead animals. So it takes all day . . . and we don't meet up until half past nine at night . . . and it's only now we start to dig ourselves in.

Bert *freezes*

Merry *unfreezes*

[**Merry** *re-stacks his ration boxes to create the seat of his army lorry, talking to the audience as he does so. Once he has finished constructing the seat he can sit in it*]

[**Bert, Cookey, Hank** *&* **Smudger** *are still in shadow*

Merry My favourite groceries are beans. Tins of baked beans! Well, with me carting rations, there's often the odd tin that falls out like, you know? [*He winks & chuckles*] They fall out and roll – whassiname – under the seat! It's only a little space, but it's big enough to get about three

Merry (*cont.*) tins in! Yeah. You can always find a tin of
beans. Beans on toast sometimes, when the bread comes
in. We don't get much bread, it's all biscuits. 'cause bread
don't keep . . . As long as I get a case of beans and . . .
[*laughs*] half of that goes in me locker where I keep me
tools – [*joking*] two spanners and a screwdriver [*winks*]
– I'm 'appy! [*Chuckles*] [*He may mime starting the engine,
driving. There should be no sound effect for this*] You ain't
got the faintest idea where ya' goin'. [*Laughs*] Red Caps
keep you on the road. They won't let you turn off. Red
Caps are the army – well, the army police and they're at
any road, so you can't turn off, so you just go through as
far as they tell ya, then go see the Sergeant Major and say
"Where do you want these?" [*As Sergeant Major*] "Stack
'em down there!" he'll say. [*As himself*] "Oh, thank you
very much, where's me help then?" [*As Sergeant Major,
shaking his fist & shouting angrily/laughing*] "You'll get
some bloody help *alright!*"

Merry *freezes shaking his fist*

Bert *unfreezes*

[**Bert** *marks out two parallel sides of a two-man trench with
ammo crates*]

[**Hank**, **Cookey** & **Smudger** *are still in shadow*

Bert So the ideal trench is – there's two of you and you dig
down and you've got two walls and you leave enough for
a step and then you sit on that. [*He climbs into the 'trench'
and sits on the step*] And then when there's a bombardment
going you watch each other . . . and if you're a smoker –
I stick a pencil in me mouth, I sometimes hold a pencil
and the fact you're holding something seems to be a bit
of relief . . . but in the morning – when there's dew on the
ground – the sergeant come round, puts five cigs for you
into the mud or grass, come round every morning – five

cigs – [*laughs*] you see cigarettes before food sometimes!
[*Pause*] For a couple of days we're in this trench that the
Germans have built, it's one of their defence trenches . . .
and we find this farming implement and it makes a sort
of shelf across the trench. But also there's a couple of
German grey coats. It's summertime so we aren't that
cold but we put the coats on top of this (shelf). So we
have a bit of warmth in that direction. [**Bert** *jumps up
anxiously*] And now, we're going into action, God willing.
We're getting ready to move off to attack the Château
de la Londe, which the Germans have taken possession
of. And erm you know we're all prepared, well our little
kit bags are put in the pile, they're going to be carried
on the truck and given to us later. We're just going to go
with our armour. We're waiting to move off, just waiting
for the, whatever it is a whistle or something. [*Whistle
blows*] [*Beat*] And then the Germans mortar us. [*Sound
of heavy mortar/distorted sounds*] And so you just dive
into a trench, the nearest one er and er as I'm falling
I feel a kick in my wrist and I fall in on two men – my
friend Mitch is one of them and there's blood coming
down me, coming down on my – and they don't know
what's happening – they can see blood coming down but
they don't know where it's [*laughs*] coming from. I say
"Look there's a bit of bandage in my pocket" and I give
it to them. They say "You go back to the First Aid Post,"
which is down the road somewhere. So I'm going back
to the First Aid Post and er, I'm being given a drug, I'm
put on a drug and being taken to the beach and we're
sleeping on the beach – all night in a tented hospital
[*surprised*] with sheets and everything. And this is only
two weeks after landing – when we're getting ready to
go into action. And I'm lying here in a tented hospital
while my comrades are getting to attack the chateau!
I'm missing out on the action again! It's going to be a
tough fight but it's vital, if we can get in, capture it . . . .
[*Beat*] I've two pieces of shrapnel in the wrist – so I can't
even fire a rifle. And the next thing I'm on a boat back,
back home, and coming in to England, we're getting off

Bert (*cont.*) the boat and there's a big welcome! In some cases it's people in the course of their work, but in other cases they appear to know the injured are coming back from France and they're there to greet you! [*Beat*] I, I say to a station master, um, somewhere near Guildford, I give him a paper with a telephone number on and I say "Can you phone that number and tell 'em Bert's wounded?"

[*Light fades on* **Bert** *leaving him in shadow*

[*In the distance, we hear the upbeat sound of a woman's voice singing* Wish me Luck as you wave me goodbye. *The song – optimistically – drives forward into safer water, and underscores* **Merry**'s *speech*]

Merry *unfreezes*

[**Bert, Cookey, Hank** *and* **Smudger** *are in shadow*

[**Merry** *is still at the wheel of his truck. He pulls up, puts the hand brake on and addresses us.*]

Merry You have to unload the truck and stack the rations in the field for them and the guys come and pick it up. 'cos the rations is all in boxes – in wooden boxes like that. [*He uses his hands to indicate the size of ration box*] And there's enough for twelve men, each box contains enough for twelve men. [*Pause*] Sometimes they like to brag a bit about what action they're seeing out 'ere, the men do . . . I let 'em go on for 'alf an 'our then I remind them they'd do bugger all if they hadn't got the ammunition or the rations . . . without me and me lorry they wouldn't get to do nothin'! [*Pause*] I getta see plenty of France and Belgium. They just give us two or three days what they term a rest, like, 'cause we've been moved up and up and up.

[*The song grows louder*]

Merry One of the singers come – was it Gracie Fields? – and we have a concert . . . one of the top what's 'er names and I'm seeing her 'ere! We take our own chair with us like to the concert so we can sit down. I mean she has a good reception like! We just have a few days off – what they call a 'rest-bite.' We go to Denmark, we go Friday Saturday Sunday and come back Monday. We just have a few days off to, you know, let ourselves go. [*Winks*] Spend the weekend drinking and making love. Drinking and making love. [*He prepares to start the truck again*] That is – you know – 'til they move you back up again.

[*The song fades out and the soundtrack kicks in again driving forward into more turbulent water*]

Lighting crossfades leaving **Merry** *and his truck in shadow and revealing* **Smudger** *on the battlefield*

[**Bert, Cookey, Hank** *and* **Merry** *are in shadow*

Smudger We live in a slit trench. Every time you stop you start to dig in, so everybody carries a pick or a shovel as well as an entrenching tool and you dig slit trenches four foot long, four foot deep, two foot wide, two people in there, you might start to dig then move on maybe three or four times a day, but one of you stands to and one of you just gets down and tries to get some sleep. So you do everything in there including toileting – you use anything you have in the slit trench and throw it out 'cos you daren't leave 'cos there's snipers out there – in five months I never sleep undercover, I never get to sit on a toilet and never sit down for a meal. You never make friends because whoever you might be sharing a trench with you might be talking to one minute – he's dead the next – it's a constant . . . you never even get to know their names, and after a few weeks you see people holding one hand up when it's heavy shelling hoping to get shell

Smudger (*cont.*) splinters, to keep them away from the front. [*Beat*] What people don't realise is that D-Day isn't the be all and end all of . . . it's far worse after. The beach is just a matter of getting off the boat and getting a little inland. The battle starts when you get into the country-side. I mean in an offensive you're probably getting half a million shells, mortars and the worst are airbursts.

[*Sound of mortar fire collides with distorted grinding sounds.* **Bert, Cookey, Hank** and **Merry** *begin whistling* Grand Old Duke of York – *a darker version, almost like a funeral march – they underscore* **Smudger***'s speech*]

Smudger (*cont.*) July 10th, we're near Caen, at Hill 112 . . . it's a high point, the hill, it's a high point – whoever holds that – the Germans won't let it go because they command the whole of Normandy right down to Caen and um . . . we're going up with three hundred odd, three hundred and twenty-eight fighting men. [**Bert, Cookey, Hank** *and* **Merry** *stop whistling abruptly*] You've got machine guns either side – the Germans have let us get halfway across then they [*stops speaking with the horror of what happens*] . . . this is far worse than D-Day. Going uphill and a shell hits a tree – it splinters it and you've got a huge sharp splinter coming down – [*stops himself*] . . . see this is the sort of violent deaths you're getting. There's seventy-ton Tiger tanks and Panthers firing at us and all you've got is a Sten gun or a rifle. I mean even our anti-tank guns just bounce off, the shells are just bouncing off – they can't knock them out. [*Pause*] This is something I shouldn't be telling you . . . we run back. [*Beat*] Their 88 millimetre guns go through our tanks and into another one, straight through . . . we're having to bury these dead within these tanks, their bodies have melted into . . . When you think four or five men in a tank, all together in a restricted area, with the guns and ammunition, and a German 88 shell coming right through, I mean I have to literally scrape the remains of a burial party, because the body – the heat of a tank that's been in flames, the body has melted onto the – it's a dreadful job to be doing . . . sometimes as an infantryman, you think it'd be great to have cover from inside a tank, but one hit and it's very few people who ever get out of them. No, it's like a steel prison. A steel tomb. In fact the Germans call them Tommy-Cookers. [*Pause*]

[*In the distance perhaps, very quietly, as if carried on the breeze, we hear the sound of a young boy singing the first three lines of* Grand Old Duke of York]

Young Boy [*offstage, singing*] Oh the Grand Old Duke of York, He had ten thousand men, He marched them up to the top of the hill...

Smudger Our unit on 112 . . . three hundred and twenty-eight fighting men and after nineteen hours only sixty of us come down . . . only sixty – we lose all those men.

[*A moment of silence . . .*]

[*Lights fade on* **Smudger** *leaving him in shadow*

[**Bert, Cookey, Hank, Merry** *&* **Smudger** *are now in shadow*

[*A drum march is heard approaching. At first it might appear as gun fire or explosion*]

[*Light fades up optimistically*]

Merry, Smudger, Cookey *and* **Bert** *jump up*

[**Bert** *picks up and places one of his crates in the middle of the stage.* **Merry, Cookey** *&* **Smudger** *grab* **Hank** *and frogmarch him to stand on the crate. This is done with good humour – barrack room banter*]

[**Bert, Cookey, Merry** *and* **Smudger** *stand either side of* **Hank** *and recite the following ditty about him, to the audience*]

Bert, Cookey, Merry *and* **Smudger** [*chanting*] "You can always tell a Guardsman, wherever he may be!

    In London or in Aberdeen or Birchington-on-Sea!

    The way he squares his shoulders. The way he wears his cap,

    The way he sits a pretty girl upon his massive lap!" [*All five men roar with laughter*]

[**Bert, Cookey, Merry** *and* **Smudger** *return to the shadows*

Hank [*with anticipation, stepping down from the crate, nervously addressing the audience*] When I'm called up I get instructions to 'present' myself at the General Service Corps at Caterham. My pal, Alan Clark – who knows about these things – says that that's the Guards Depot! The *Coldstream* Guards! ... you know it can't possibly be the Guards, 'cos I'm a weakling, you know, five foot ten, and only weigh about eight stone – at school the welfare report says I'm malnourished – well me mother and father, what with being deaf and dumb, they can't get much of a job, so I'm very, very thin ... I'm a bit immature you know, a bit shy, reserved and, you know, I don't get on at school – 'cos I don't really think I'm much good – and the teacher always seems very anxious to use her cane on me wherever possible! – so the last thing I expect is to be selected for the Coldstream Guards! [*Pause*] It's twelve weeks of very tough discipline. Everything's done at the double but now I'm feeling really fit. Fitter than I've ever been and full of confidence and [*amused astonishment*] I weigh ten and a half stone! [*With surprise*] And I'm commended for my shooting! The weapons instructor writes in my small arms handbook, "A good man and a good shot, needs no coaching." Up to this stage we've been referred to as 'recruits' but now we can call ourselves 'Guardsmen.' We parade and march with full kit down to Caterham Station for Waterloo! [*Pause*] At the Armoured Training

wing at Pirbright we take over our first Sherman Tanks!
There's five of us in a tank. Five that's right: a driver a
co-driver, a gunner – that's me – a co-gunner and the
tank commander. The first tank I drive is a Covenanter. I
get to the top of the hill but the tank careers backwards
down the hill for about fifty yards and hits a tree! We
are all shaken – including the instructor! Then, driving
a Crusader for the first time on the roads we have a
sharp corner to turn, and the instructor tells me to rev
up and pull sharply on the left tiller, but the tank goes
straight across the road and demolishes a brick letter
box! [*Pause*] After a few weeks of beautiful sunshine we
move our tanks to Duncombe Park, Helmsley and spend
the first of the summer here. We don't know then how
similar this area is to the Bocage country in France. [*His
nervous excitement building*] And now today, the 30th of
June, we're moving off to Gosport with our tanks – ready
to cross the Channel. People are lining the route and
cheering and arm waving. And sitting here on the boat
I'm trying to take in the spectacle of hundreds of boats
and ships of all sizes . . . Darkness comes and we begin to
move off to Normandy. Our first stop is going to be Tilly
sur Seulles. [*Beat*] There's hardly a wall standing. The
whole town has been completely devastated. A terrible
sight. German defence trenches and inside enormous
numbers of dead German soldiers, all bloated and blue
with the heat, and bloody holes in their chests and faces.
Of those whose faces are visible you can see expressions
of fear and pain. The smell coming from the trenches
and from the cows and horses which've been killed is
absolutely horrible. [*Long pause*] It's an unmistakeable
smell, the smell of death.

Lighting cross fades to reveal **Merry** *in his lorry, driving*

[*Sounds of people cheering and clapping, beeping horns of army
vehicles momentarily*]

[**Bert**, **Cookey**, **Hank** *and* **Smudger** *are now in shadow*

Merry I'm the third man, the third man into Antwerp
– after what they call the supply famine – the British
troops had started to suffer from supply problems –
'cos they're pushing on up toward Germany, faster than
they'd planned and the only way the supply famine can
end is if the British liberate the port'a Antwerp. And
now here I am, the third man in! There's a driver first,
then Cap'n, and then it's me. So I'm the third man in
here! I'm 'avin a job to go down the ruddy streets 'cos
they've been under German rule 'ere and they're out
on the streets clappin' [*laughs*] and that, it's, well I'm
'avin' a job to, 'avin' a job to get through like 'cos if I
speed up I'll have somebody run over like, you know!
[*Sound of people cheering and clapping fades away*] The
lads are 'specially pleased when you turn up, 'cos you
got food on! I mean when you got all their rations on
they're always pleased to see you! Rations and cigarettes
– cigarettes are more important than food actually. You
can always do with a cigarette. [*Searches his pockets. Goes to
light a cigarette. Stops. Remembers*]

[*The youthful voices of choirboys can be heard in the distance
singing the hymn,* I vow to thee my country *– an uplifting
song, carried in on a breeze before dissipating again, or gently
underscoring*]

Merry When we was kids like, me brother John was a
choirboy back home at Stratford. Now they used to sell
two Crown cigarettes and two matches in a box when
we was little. [*Confidentially. Grinning*] We go buy, buy
a packet, and we go up, sit up in the rafters 'cos uh,
nobody can smell you when you're up in the whas-a-
name, it's perfect! . . . never think about 'ow 'igh the
bloody thing is! It's only about sixty, eighty foot high!
[*Bursts out laughing*] But no never think about how high
the bloody thing is! [*Wistfully*] Just sit up there 'aving a
smoke!

[*The hymn finishes*] [*Beat*] [*The church bell tolls – once. An
omen*]

[*Lights cross fade to reveal* **Cookey** *and* **Smudger** – *in their separate battalions* – *on the move. Their movements are low, slow and cautious. They might mime carrying a weapon, as they look around furtively with each step. It should be clear that they are not in the same place together but in their separate battalions in different parts of Normandy*]

[**Bert**, **Hank** *and* **Merry** *remain in shadow*

Cookey [*confidentially*] We're to find out how many Germans are in the village, where they are and what tactics we have to use to clear them out, whether we go round from different angles to clear them out and if er there's any . . . if they don't want to be cleared out, we . . . we have to fight them and you know er do it that way. I don't have time to be afraid. You know, just, oh, what's going on here? Keep going, keep going. Orders from – "A sniper up there, stop here, right we've cleared him all the way, carry on." And that's how we advance, one after the other.

Smudger [*confidentially*] There's plenty of food in Normandy – they aren't starving like in Paris. And by and large the Germans have been behaving themselves here – but I mean there's been *some* atrocities, massacres in villages – perhaps in retaliation for a German Officer that's been killed and you come across villagers locked into village halls and set on fire, you know, burnt alive. You go to a farm and there's the farmer, his wife and his children spreadeagled across the courtyard, some of the times they've been killed by retreating Germans or they've been caught in the crossfire . . . the battles you see are mainly farm to farm. And we're advancing through this village and we see a furtive head pop up – the civilians are here in the cellars, they've not just evacuated, they're still here! And there's two German tiger tanks in the Square being re-armed from an ammunition truck and the Commander's ordering us to fire everything we have at this! But hang on, the French civilians are still here, amidst the battle. We're being

Smudger (*cont.*) commanded to "Open fire" – but there's
civilians! Only a few shots ring out and we're being
threatened with a court martial, severe punishment –
because we've held our fire. He's giving us a final warning
and we have to open fire. We have to. The first two-inch
mortar blows the ammunition truck up, nothing left of
it, one tank ablaze – getting out of the way as quick as
you can. But these French people they can't get out of
the way. They're still in the cellars of their houses, and
their houses are being obliterated. I think some of us
might . . . mis-aim, but you can't afford – if the enemy
infiltrates into your lines . . . well sometimes you have to
call down your own artillery to keep it secure.

This is why the Battle of Normandy is so important –
apart from liberating these villages there's the people
back home – if we fail that'll be it – *we'll* be under
German rule. I mean who can come to rescue us from
the Nazis? There's no one left in Europe that can do it.
Europe's conquered.

[*The church bell tolls again*]

[*Lights cross fade to reveal night time*]

We see **Merry** *sitting on his lorry seat again*

[**Bert, Cookey, Hank** *and* **Smudger** *are in shadow*

Merry I ain't lookin for danger. You do as Sergeant tells ya
and ya try not to think about how a road might be booby
trapped or if there's a panther waiting round the corner
like. And tonight, yeah? I'm out, and I run, I run outta
petrol! I'm outta petrol, and this German pops up outta
this hedge! And he's got a revolver in his hand. I say to him
"Red Cross! Red Cross!" like, you know? "I don't have
nothing like!" And I'm tryin'a' make 'im understand.
[*Looking to where he 'sees' the German soldier*] "Red Cross!"
and off he goes! . . . Thank Gawd! [*Composing himself
again and addressing the audience*] So I'm going back, back

to headquarters and I'm coming down this back road and I see something in the whassiname in the shadow ahead, and I get to the corner – it's a Tiger tank – nearly poop meself! Shoot round the corner and open 'er up! I mean when you come down the road and just see it sticking out, see that gun turret sticking out – you get outta there!

[*Soundtrack carries the momentum forward as light crossfades to spotlight*]

Cookey *jumps up salutes and stands to attention in spotlight to read a telegram*

[*Sound of airbursts/ distorted sound or a drum march permeate the following speech*]

[**Bert, Hank, Merry** *and* **Smudger** *may place the blocks to create steps up to a front door on which* **Cookey** *might knock before saluting and speaking*]

[**Bert, Hank, Merry** *and* **Smudger** *retreat to shadow*

Cookey [*reading*] "Infantry Record Office, July 1944. Sir/Madam, I regret to have to inform you that a report has been received War Office to the effect that Number 14693549, Private Cooke, Kenneth Basil, 7th Green Howards is dangerously ill at 79 General Hospital suffering from bomb wounds, back, and left leg, at the same time to express the sympathy and regret of the Army Council. Any further information as his condition has progressed will be notified to you. I am, Madam your obedient servant The Officer in Charge of Records." [*He salutes, then relaxes, jumps down and addresses us as lights cross fade to daytime*] July 14th. Been 'ere just over a month. I'm on patrol in a hedgerow. This shell comes over, hits a tree and splatters all of us who are down below, about fifteen, sixteen of us. Now I don't know how many are killed or wounded but I'm wounded myself – shrapnel all in me back and leg and er, and two more

Cookey (*cont.*) chaps come and pick me up and take me
back to the First Aid station. And the next thing I know
this circle of light, from then on all there is, is a circle of
light, which tells me I'm on the operating table. I wake
up, lying on me stomach in the field hospital with a nurse
sticking needles in me bum. Quite a wake-up call, I can
tell ya! [*Laughs*] They're coming every hour with these
needles. And I'm getting fed up. I get to a stage, tears are
rolling. I say "No, not again!" And I'm lying there, in this
big marquee that's the field hospital, with all beds and er
nurses and doctors running about – and the opening of
the marquee at the far end, like two flaps, is open . . . and
these two Germans are walking across the opening, and
I shout to the nurse "Where's me rifle?" She says "What
for?" [*As himself*] "There's two Germans out there!" [*As
nurse, mock whispers her response behind his hand*] "They're
two medical staff of the Germans who are helping us,
helping our staff!" [*Beat. As himself, addressing the audience
again*] Prisoners of war! And there's me [*mimes holding
rifle*] wanting to pump them up!

[*The soundtrack breaks into less perilous waters*

Lighting cross fades into afternoon to reveal **Hank**

Hank *picks up an ammo box and stands it end up on top of
other crates. He will use it to demonstrate how to make a cup
of tea. The ammo box will represent the jerry can. He may use
a small military stick or a twig to point to different areas of the
jerry can in his demonstration. His delivery of these instructions
to us is somewhere between imitating one of his superior officers
giving instructions for a military operation to his men, and a
celebrity chef carrying out a cooking demonstration on a live
cookery show*]

Hank "How to make a cup of tea whilst on the move."
[*Picking up ammo box on which to demonstrate*] Take one
petrol tin – a square one, not a jerry can and cut in two.
Fill one half with earth and onto that pour a bit of petrol,

then, get a match and set it alight. Then on top of this goes the other half – which you need to fill with water. Bring to the boil and add tea – or rather Compo! [*As himself*] When we're on the move we get the tins out whenever we stop and make a cup of tea. Well it's not normal tea – it's horrible stuff – it's called Compo, 'cos it's a composition of tea, sugar and milk powder – horrible . . . but better than nothing. There's this one time we're near a battery of 5.5 Howitzers south of Caen – which, by the way, has been really badly damaged – and we're just finishing a cup of Compo when out of nowhere this shell comes over and explodes right near our makeshift toilet – on which one of our men just happens to be sitting! [*Laughing*] And as we're running for cover we see him jump up and he's dashing across to his tank with his trousers round his ankles, trying to restore them to their normal position as explosions are still going off behind him! [**Hank** *stops laughing. Distorted sounds permeate.* **Hank** *sits on the assembled crates from the demo – they become the seat inside the tank*] We're going into action again and to tell you the truth I'm not looking forward to it. It's August 10th and our troop is up the hill in an orchard supporting a battalion of Irish Guards who are trying to take the road between Vire and Vassy – a very strategic road. [*Worried*] We're moving off down the hill – in full view of the enemy . . . Several tanks have already been knocked out – shell and mortar fire everywhere and I'm firing at spots of light on the opposite hillside. The empty shell cases are clattering down on the steel floor of the turret, the noise of gunfire and voices on the radio and intercom through our headphones, it's bedlam! We've never seen on exercise what gunfire looks like when it's directed at us! [*Beat*] Suddenly the tank shudders, but it's okay and we're carrying on. It shudders again. Suddenly the shell pierces the gun mounting shield and pieces of the inside of the tank armour break away and are flying around the tank piercing my arm and face and even smaller pieces pepper my chest. We've got to get out – but it's hurting so much and I'm looking down and it looks like my, my,

Hank (*cont.*) my arm is lying on the floor of the turret! [*Beat*]
We're getting out as fast as we can and congregating at
the rear of the tank. My arm's bleeding profusely but we
have to start running for cover – across to a hedge – and
we, we, we follow the line of it. There's shell and mortar
fire all around us and we're passing Irish Guardsmen in
slit trenches, poor devils but we have to, to, to keep going,
me in the lead. [*Stops speaking as he notices*] "Two German
soldiers behind a machine gun hidden in the hedge, Sir!"
The officer's going forward . . . [*watches*] and it's alright,
he's signalling for us to come forward – the soldiers are
dead – and we're carrying on and we're following the
hedge left out of sight of the enemy and it's only now
we stop and they're dressing my bleeding wound. I'm
reaching in my left breast pocket next to my heart to
find my cigarettes and [*surprised*] the case has two holes
through it, and my army prayer book, and I'm looking at
them, looking at the two holes, at my bleeding arm, and
at my heart, thinking, thinking, these, [*indicating cigarettes
& army prayer book*] these have just saved my life.

[*Soundtrack underscores gently as if carried in on a distant
breeze – overlaid by a soulful, haunting version of a woman
singing* Wish me luck as you wave me goodbye, *her heart
breaking as she sings*]

Hank And the next thing I'm being taken to the field
hospital and they're wheeling me into theatre –
removing splinters from my arm but they can't get all of
them and they're saying I have to go back to England.
More surgery here will probably damage the muscle of
my arm. And a nurse is leaning over me removing the
peppered pieces from my chest and face. [*Relief kicks in*]
And I'm on my way home, and I can see the faces of
crowds of people cheering as we're arriving back home
and a huge banner waving in the wind – [*with modest
surprise*] 'Welcome to our heroes of Normandy.'

[*The song increases in volume and then slowly fades out as the
action reaches:*

Four
The Last Push

Holland **1944**

Bert *is alone on night patrol*

[**Hank**, **Cookey**, **Smudger** *&* **Merry** *are in shadow –*
elsewhere in Europe or at home

Bert I think I'm having an easy war in some ways . . . I
come back to the regiment after four months being
wounded. Eventually we go back into Holland around
Christmas time and I catch up with the battalion but a
different company this time – the 'C' Company. [*Pause*]
The winter is coming. You're not fighting all the time.
You sometimes go in the front line for three, well, two
weeks maybe. [**Bert** *listens to the silence. All quiet*] There's
this one time, we're in this place – if you can imagine a
gully, a countryside gully – and the sides are going up a
bit with the earth. And they've dug not down but into
the side of the gully, they've dug into that. So you get
on your hands and knees and you crawl, and you go in,
and it's a bit damp, mm, and you're boots are muddy
– oh dear – and you have to turn your back . . . follow?
Deep enough to stretch out – enough to put my knees
up, the earth is over you – no light, I don't even have a
torch – it's like . . . a mole hole. That's it! I imagine I'm a
mole. I feel like a mole! [*Laughs*] It's the getting in and
turning, it's horrible! It's the worst, it's the worst place. If
ever I wanted to give up it's in this hole! [*Sound of distant
shell fire.* **Bert** *responds, listens intently. Remembers*] It's night

Bert (*cont.*) time and we're on the River Maas and the Germans are on the other side. We're on our way back from nightly patrol. The sergeant has asked for volunteers – "'oo wants to go on patrol?" – and I think I'd better volunteer and we've been wandering round for two, three hours, long time, and while you're patrolling you have a grenade in your hand, and you pull the pin out. So you're holding a grenade for two or three hours, but you don't let it go [*nervous laugh*] – 'cos if you let go it'll take you out – so you make sure you're holding that tight! I mean the idea is that if you get shot at you'd throw it straightaway. I've never had to do that so far. And tonight all's quiet. And we're on our way back . . . we're making our way back through the quiet – when we get back we can put the pin back in [*laughs*] . . . and suddenly we're being fired on! [*Distorted sounds*] We're being shot at but we're too green to know what to do! And we're being fired on and we realise – from the direction – we're being shot at by our own men, we're being fired on by the English! It's our . . . we start shouting "We're 'C' Company! Where are you?" and they're shouting "We're 'D' Company" so I'm shouting "Well don't shoot us!" And we're having to negotiate with them to get back to our position! I mean the poor British Squaddie doesn't know where the other companies are – the sergeant might, the officers might, but we don't! [*Pause*] "Don't shoot us!"

[*Soundtrack kicks in*]

Cookey, **Hank**, **Merry** *and* **Smudger** *move out of shadow and join* **Bert**

[**Bert, Cookey, Hank, Merry** *and* **Smudger** *then proceed to find their own 'camps' within Europe. They might use the crates to do this – or simply commandeer different areas that the crates are already in from previous scenes, and use the crates to sit on, sit against, hide next to etc according to their situation. Where*

*before the crates may have appeared 'regimented' in how they were
stood or stacked, things may be more haphazard now reflecting
the places the soldiers find themselves – for example a ghost town
billet in Germany, the battlefield etc]*

Cookey After months in hospital in a plaster cast from
'ere to 'ere, they putting me on another plane sending
me back over, to join up with the HLI – Highland Light
Infantry! I ask why I, why I aren't going back to me own
regiment – it appears they took a pasting my regiment
at Nijmegen, they all split up the . . . the, er, other
regiments are short of men so they're taking men from
different regiments such as ours to make up numbers
and I'm to join up with the HLI in Belgium.

Hank After being declared fit again I'm given ten days
leave, but after about seven days I'm ordered to report to
Pirbright immediately. A couple of days later we're at sea
again in a landing craft, sailing for Dieppe and I re-join No
2 Squadron – and everyone's surprised to see me, including Les Hanson, saying "Hello, I thought you were dead!"
[*Pause*] We're billeted in a German Village – Hillensberg –
and all the civilians are being moved out so we can occupy
their houses – it's December now. The squadrons in the
Battalion have to take turns at holding the front line. The
area is like flat moorland but covered in a thin layer of
snow. We change places with those dug out nearer the enemy. [*Pause*] The Germans here occasionally send shells
over which hiss by, scattering leaflets all over the place.
The message on the leaflets conveys the fact that to enjoy
Christmas all we have to do is to walk forward and give
ourselves up. [*Pause*] It was my twenty-first birthday the
other week and tomorrow is Christmas Day.

[*Cross fade to winter light.* **Bert, Cookey, Hank, Merry** *and*
Smudger *begin humming the Christmas carol* Silent Night.
*Although they are stationed in different parts of Europe the
humming of a traditional carol should somehow unite them*]

[**Bert, Cookey, Hank** *and* **Smudger***'s humming underscores
as* **Merry** *reads his letter aloud*]

Merry [*taking out a scrap of paper and a pencil from his pocket, begins to write a Christmas message home*][1]

"Christmas Greeting . . .

Somebody cares a lot for you,

Wherever you are, whatever you do,

Cares if you're troubled, or ill or sad

Cares if your happy, well and glad

Somebody loves your voice, your smile

The touch of your hand what makes life worthwhile

And someday perhaps as years roll on,

You'll look behind, o'er the road we've gone,

Then you'll discover, by and by,

The somebody caring so much was I.

To Mum and Dad

With lots of love from your son

George"

I don't write home much. Write odd letters or two but it er, writing doesn't come easy to me so I just write a few lines to Mother, saying "I'm still alive Mother. I don't know where I am. [*Laughs*] But I'm not in England!"

Bert I spend Christmas on the River Maas and I'm one of the lucky ones, I get ten ten letters or packages from home! Amazing, wonderful, ah yes, yes.

[*The final line of* Silent Night – *Sleep in heavenly peace – can be heard*]

[*Silence*]

---

1 This letter can be found in the York Normandy Veterans' Archive.

[*This silence should contrast sharply with the intense energy of the following speeches which should build in momentum, the relentless momentum of the battlefield, as if the actors are relay racers continually passing a baton between each other, building and keeping the urgent momentum going*]

Hank [*suddenly*] We're in Neerheylissem for about six weeks suffering the noise and the silence of many a buzz bomb. You got noise then silence. Noise. Silence.

Cookey By March we're on the banks of the Rhine and we join up with the Canadians who are already here dug in.

Hank Silence then noise. Silence then noise.

[*Haze begins to creep in gently throughout the scene*]

Cookey [*jumping up, first hearing then seeing*] Suddenly we hear this noise, screaming noise – this Messerschmitt's coming down, Spitfire chases him, what a noise, they have like a siren on the tail they have a like a siren and when the air is rushing through it, it makes this screaming noise you know, whoa, [*puts his hands over his ears*] never heard anything like it! [*Beat*] We set out to cross the Rhine, er we have er these er flat bottom boats and er ours has an engine on the back, we have a motor on the back, engine on the back, there's a bit a noise as we're setting off – from the guns artillery, the noise of the engine, and then the barrage over the other side, the guns are lined up along the banks on the Rhine, five point five they are, big guns up to sixty . . . sixty to about a hundred along the Rhine boom-boom-boom-boom-boom bang bang bang . . . more noise, smoke, there's another explosion, a big explosion, fireworks and all the rest of it, and we've got to keep going, got to get across the Rhine.

Hank Silence then . . . [*Beat*] Noise. [*Beat*] Silence then –

Smudger Night comes . . . It's now October 20th and we're just beginning to enter Germany and we get a patrol in there during daylight and keep squat and observe and wait for nightfall.

[*We hear faintly a ghostly, distorted music hall rendition of* The Daring Young Man on the Flying Trapeze *which blows in on the breeze and gently underscores* **Smudger***'s speech. His speech builds in intensity as his recollections come to life around him – the audience is there in the trench with him seeing what he sees*]

Smudger I'm dug in near the bridge and there's a wood opposite us and there's two of us, I've another chap with me, another soldier. We know there's some armour in there. I mean shells have a terrific range, up to twenty miles some of the bigger guns. You're never really safe anywhere. I'm getting out the slit trench when suddenly they're firing – and a shell bursts very close to me and the blast takes me off my feet and I'm flying through the air with the greatest of ease [*laughs*] blowing me into a previous RAF bomb crater so the German tanks can no longer see me.

[*The sound fades out as the music hall audience cheer and clap*]

Smudger And the other poor chap [*sees him, indicates where he is*] – I'm so lucky, because I'm nearer to it – the shell bursts very close to me but the chap ten yards from me is killed. When a shell bursts it kills two ways, one is the blast and blast will disarrange your insides but not leave a mark on you – but you're dead. Or the shrapnel when it bursts comes up and over and hits somebody further away. [*Nods in the other chap's direction*] He's dead. [*A long pause*] And the shrapnel comes through here [*indicates*] into my left thigh and lower abdomen – the biggest bit lodges in my hip. And looking down, all the front of my battle dress is absolutely soaked in blood – and I'm thinking I must've been – I must be disembowelled – there's so much blood. And next thing I'm bumping down this road on a, a jeep with two outriggers that carry four stretchers on them and I pass Battalion headquarters perhaps half a mile down the road and a voice comes across "You lucky so and so, Smudger!" – they know – I'm getting out of it!

Hank [*building on the energy and intensity of* **Smudger***'s* *speech –* **Hank** *finds himself back in the frontline and anxiously describes, at speed, the action as it happens around him*] It's April 1st – not only Easter Sunday but April Fool's Day and we're the leading battalion. Our squadron is the leading squadron, and we are the leading troop, and our tank is the leading tank . . . the first tank. [*Beat*] Our objective is to capture a bridge over a large canal at Enschede and stop the Germans in their tracks. And we're approaching the bridge, but there's a huge bomb on each corner of it. Our tank commander's reporting the bombs to the Squadron HQ on the radio but we're still being ordered to cross the bridge to form a bridgehead, and we're crossing the bridge at full speed and I'm praying the bombs won't be detonated before we get across! [*Breathes*] All three tanks get across before there's a terrible *whoof* of an explosion. The bridge has been blown and we're, we're isolated from our squadron. I'm being ordered to fire my Browning .303 at everything I can see – all windows in the flats down the road – anything that moves. [*Beat*] Suddenly a German army bus is coming towards us. I fire at the bus and it turns sharp right. Soldiers are jumping off the bus as it turns and I'm obliged to fire at them as they're running for cover. I spot a German with a bazooka in the field to our right, but I can't bring my machine gun to bear on him and I'm reporting to Lieutenant Jardine but before he can turn the turret the bazooka fires at us and our right-hand track breaks and the tank's hurtling off the road onto the embankment of the bridge. [*Recovering quickly and carrying on*] We're evacuating the tank as quick as we can and we're hurrying down, shielded by the embankment, down to the water. We have to get back to our regiment but that means we're going to have to swim across a river, 'cos the bridge has been blown – but I can't swim, can I? And further down the canal and beyond the bridge we can see Germans crossing to our side in a small boat! The others are swimming across, but I can't swim! Lieutenant Jardine is trying to persuade me to go as far as I can with his help. [*Terrified*]

Hank (*cont.*) I'm wading in the water and then suddenly
thank God I can feel the balustrade of the bridge below
the surface – it's rather a funny experience because
under the water – with my feet – I can feel the handrail
of the bridge that's been blown up – and it's bringing
me to safety. [*Beat*] We're clambering onto the other
shore, without our boots and jackets, absolutely wet
through and freezing and we're running in single file
along the bottom of the embankment and suddenly
there's Mr Boscawen's tank as we're coming to the road.
[*Hank stops speaking/stops dead in his tracks*] The tank is
ablaze. [*Pause*] I shall never forget the horrific sight of
Les Hanson's corpse burning on the back of that tank.
Strangely he is lying on his back in a sitting position.
Tug Wilson and Bradbury are also dead. The Officer
Mr Boscawen and Bland the driver are severely burned.
We have run across a minefield from the bridge and are
being fired on all the way. [*Disbelief*] None of us are hit.
[*Recovering and carrying on*] We keep going and we're
trying to throw ourselves on the back of Mr Sedgewick's
tank and he's taking us to a place of safety – a Dutch
farmhouse – and the Sergeant Major's pouring us drinks
and giving us dry clothes and the next thing we're
moving back to Enschede to join the squadron and we
get there and suddenly they're saying [*disbelief*] that the
squadron has gone into a German village called Berg.
Unknown to them German Paratroopers are hiding in
the upstairs rooms of the village and as our tanks have
filled the main street they've fired down on them.

Fire.

Fire down on them.

All dead.

Every single last one . . . dead. [*Beat*]

Everything's spinning and my knees are buckling and
I'm sitting on a petrol jerry can in a semi-conscious state.
All the rest of our squadron. Dead. Why do we have to

kill each other? All these poor people, killed. It's daft! The Sergeant Major's taking me to the Company Orders and the Squadron Commander's suggesting that being knocked out of two tanks is enough for anyone and he's asking me if I would be willing to be a batmun? As far as I am concerned anything is better than going back into one of those 'Galvanised Messtins.' But I can't. I can't, Sir. I can't abandon my comrades.

Cookey [*maintaining the momentum*] We fight our way up towards Bremen. We see some towns absolutely flattened, you know? You know, all these artillery just flatten houses and different buildings and all that. And we're just outside Bremen, we're nearly there . . . we get into these positions – trenches what are already, Germans already dug, we get into them, hide in them . . . [*quietly – he is back there*] and we're hiding in them . . . and there's a road on our right- hand side and we spot two Germans coming towards us, coming towards the trench, so we wait for 'em coming round this hedge, and we're up and shouting at 'em to "Put down your weapons!" One of them's running, running like the blazes down field and, er there must be a dozen of us firing at him, and none of us none of us hit him! The other chap he's putting his hands up like . . . [*Beat*] Next day, silence. All quiet. All quiet. [*Building in intensity*] Whether the one who escaped told about us – (that) we'd be up this end, I don't know but er – suddenly we getting this barrage of artillery on us, firing on us, bang bangbang firing on us, bang bangbangbang firing, firing, firing on and on and on – firing rockets, the Nebelwerfers scream as they're coming through putting the fear of God in us, smoke, noise, explosions, like fireworks, noise, noise, noise going off all around me, everywhere and the explosions are making me,

make me

made me

a bit doolally you know?

[*Beat*]

[*The following speech should be delivered in keeping with what has just happened to* **Cookey**]

Cookey My mum receives a letter.[1]

"Infantry Record Office. 2nd May 1945, Infantry Records, Perth.

Dear Madam,

Number 14693549, Private Cooke, Kenneth Basil Highland Light Infantry have to inform you that Private *above named soldier* was reported missing / kidnapped / prisoner of war in Western Europe April 1945."

Silence.

[**Bert**, **Cookey**, **Hank**, **Merry** *&* **Smudger** *remain in silence*]

[*Fade to blackout*

[*The haze begins to fade away. After a moment the soundtrack kicks in pushing forward into the cold light of day and . . .*

---

1 This telegram can be found in the York Normandy Veterans' Archive

Five
The end approaches

[**Bert**, **Cookey**, **Hank**, **Merry** and **Smudger** *stand at ease amid the strewn crates. Although the end is in sight their mood is subdued. They are exhausted*]

Smudger I've had five months before I get wounded, and it's the happiest day of my life, 'cos it gets me out from the constant shelling . . . because after several months you begin to get, uh, it's not shell shock but we used to say we're bomb happy. And I just feel that starting in myself. Battle fatigue is accepted in the American Army, a very high proportion of their fighting men are invalided away from the front with battle fatigue but it isn't accepted in the British – there are people who after a few months – everybody has a different rate of . . . some can stand more than others. It isn't the toughest chap that can stand it, and it's not the bravery, it's the having to do it, no choice. And when I'm bumping past headquarters on that stretcher it's the happiest day of my life.

Hank The end of hostilities isn't far away. Though the war is over for the country – the agreed date is May 8th – we don't get to come home. We don't see VE Day.

Smudger The end of the war in Europe doesn't mean the end of the war for us and once I'm out of hospital we're sent out on the troop ship *The Strathmore* to Palestine.

Bert I'm two years in Germany after the war – the battalion is to be sent to Palestine but the officer says "You're going to Rhine Army Headquarters."

Merry It's five years before they let me come 'ome again. After I get out, I try looking for Bill and Stooart again. That's when I learn Stooart got shot – two days before the end of the war. [*Pause*] I never find Bill.

Hank It's not 'til February 1947 I'm demobbed – given my demob suit, shirt and overcoat. I'm twenty-three. Before I leave Caterham, Captain Jessel writes in my discharge papers: 'Military Conduct – Exemplary. This is the most admirable man who is honest, intelligent and thoroughly reliable. He can be relied on to fill any position of trust. He will go a long way in civilian life.' [*Pause*] The shrapnel splinters are still in my arm.

Cookey I turn up in a transit hospital with shellshock. What they later call 'Post Traumatic Stress Disorder.' The discharge doctor takes one look at the scars all over my back and legs from my previous injury and tells me 'You should never've been sent back, son,' he says, 'you should never have been sent back out there.'

Smudger After five long years conscripted, I arrive back in York carrying my de-mob suit and I walk to the station, instead of getting an army truck and I call in at um at the nearest church – and I kneel at the altar and I take an oath that I will never handle another weapon again. And, not even a toy one, or at a shooting gallery, and that if I am ever recalled to the colours. I will literally refuse to be a combatant – I'll do anything, but I won't be a combatant. No matter what it costs. The reason being if you're behind a machine gun day after day you're responsible for killing and wounding literally hundreds of people. And as time goes by it doesn't get any easier to think what you've done. What you were made to do. [*Beat*] Violent death is different to er somebody who dies in hospital in a nice clean sheet. Violent death, it's something indecent, um the same as the thousands upon thousands where they, they don't know who the bodies are. They don't know where the bodies are. You know, when you know that your son or your daughter, your loved one is, is nowhere. [*Beat*] Not just a thousand killed, but twenty, thirty, forty thousand in unmarked graves. [*Clears throat*] And, er, the terrible things that some of those lads went through – I mean, um, you can't, you can't get it over to people.

Cookey People say we're heroes when we come back.
We're not. The lads over there . . . the ones who never
came back, they're the heroes.

[*As the soundtrack kicks in* **Bert**, **Cookey**, **Hank**, **Merry** *and*
Smudger *pick up the crates, their movements slow and heavy –
almost in slow motion, they begin to pass and carry the ammo
boxes and ration crates back to the large army crate. When the
final crate is placed inside the soldiers will stop for a moment and
acknowledge each other's presence – this might just be through eye
contact or a slight nod. Then together they will close the crate lid
shut fast*]

[*The light will fade down on* **Bert**, **Cookey**, **Hank**, **Merry** *and*
Smudger *in tableaux – perhaps reminiscent of a war memorial –
around the large crate – but it will not extinguish them – we will
still be aware of them, almost as ghosts*]

A spotlight reveals **Queenie** *downstage from* **Bert**, **Cookey**,
Hank, **Merry** *and* **Smudger**

Queenie [*addressing the audience*] June 6th this year is
probably the last that the Veterans will visit (France) –
they're in their nineties now, you see, the five that are
still with us. But they were determined to go again this
year – this is the year they get presented with the *Legion
D'Honneur* Medal – the highest accolade a soldier can get
in France. [*Pause*] I remember one time we were over
there in France, for the commemorations, I think it was
the seventieth anniversary, and we visited this village which
had been liberated by the British. And I'll never forget,
there was an old gentleman – he was tending a grave,
and then he saw us, saw the Veterans with their medals
on and he came across to embrace us, shake hands and
he told us he was seventeen when it happened, that day,
and his mother was killed by the shelling. The shelling
before the attack killed his mother. He was seventeen
(back then). And he comes across to embrace us, shake
hands and thank the Veterans. He thanked my husband

Queenie (*cont.*) "for helping to liberate the village and their country" he said, just like that and he was very nice, and it was very, very upsetting to listen to this – he was attending the actual grave at the time and it was so sad, well when you think to come up to a soldier that you know was partly responsible for your mother – and come and say *thank you* . . . [*she struggles to comprehend*] He doesn't sleep well, my husband. He has these moments, I get very upset when I see him have these moments because I don't want him to remember, I know he'll never forget but I don't want it to keep coming back to him. For that few minutes 'til I wake him up he's at war. And I can tell by his actions, he shouts, calling out, um [*stops herself*] . . . and things like that. He, he just doesn't like to, I don't know . . . [*Sighs, deep intake of breath, forces herself to keep going*] I don't think he likes me having to listen sometimes, but naturally I'm his wife and I want to know what he's been through . . . and all these other men, all these veterans, it must have been an horrific thing for them really. I mean to get off that landing craft knowing that, knowing what you were facing . . . I don't think I could ever have done it. I suppose as he said, you have to do it, you're conscripted at eighteen and you've no choice. You can't say "No I'm not going to do it." [*Beat*] You have no choice.

[*Choirboys singing* I vow to thee my country *underscores gently*]

Queenie What haunts him most is those left behind. The ones who at eighteen, nineteen, twenty and even younger, didn't survive. They were vibrant happy-go-lucky people, full of life. And when he goes over there to the cemeteries and he sees those names he says "I know these names, I trained with them, I've drunk with them, played football with them, landed with them and then . . . they're gone and I'm still here. And I go and get seventy more years of life – wonderful life. And I have to live with that," he says . . . "I have to live with it."

And he does. They all do. Every day.

[*A solitary chorister sings the final line from* I vow to thee my country – '*The love that makes undaunted the final sacrifice*']

[*Light fades on* **Queenie**, *leaving the tableaux of*

Bert, **Cookey**, **Hank**, **Merry** *and* **Smudger** *around the crate, lit*

[*Light slowly fades on tableaux*